the
1700s

DO
A Little Book of
EARLY AMERICAN
KNOW-HOW

Eric Sloane's

DO

a little book of early American know-how.

WALKER AND COMPANY
New York

First published in the United States of America in 1972 by the Walker Publishing Company, Inc.

Published simultaneously in Canada by Fitz-henry & Whiteside, Limited, Toronto.

ISBN: 0-8027-0388-7

Library of Congress Catalog Card Number: 70-186180

Printed in the United States of America.

—a Foreword—

Early America was cluttered with a weary lot of "don'ts." People were so strict about not doing this and not doing that. Yet that disciplined life was also livened by an amazing number of things to do. Benjamin Franklin's warning about "idle hands getting into mischief" was intended for children but there is so little for adults to do for themselves nowadays that the self-doer is nearly obsolete and modern living has become a bore.

One of the first delights of life was when the child learned to button up his own pants but the zipper eliminated that satisfying exercise of dexterity. Grinding coffee, making ice cream, shining shoes, and nearly all the small movements that made up the continuous ballet of daily life a few years back are now being done by plugging into a socket or flipping a switch. Even the satisfaction of knowing where that electric power comes from is kept from us and sometimes the power company doesn't know either. I still recall the extraordinary pleasure of pumping spring water and carrying it for the household: now I turn on a faucet and I am too lazy to wonder where the stuff is coming from. Perhaps if I really knew, I wouldn't drink it. We used to pray to God for our needs to be fulfilled; now we depend upon the establishment.

Years ago when I contemplated the difference between the early American and his modern counterpart, I made some interesting finds. The old-timer was smaller, about twenty to fifty pounds lighter than the average man of today, but he was wiry and very much stronger.

Bread was as solid and hard as the people who ate it, but now the "staff of life" is as fat and spongy and full of air as we have become. The "sports fan" of today seldom does his own thing; instead, he watches others do their things, eating and drinking at the TV while sitting on a behind that would have shamed great-grandfather.

There is no doubt about it, doing things by and for ourselves has become a lost art, and the joy of doing things not just "the old-fashioned way" but plainly the right way is a nearly vanished satisfaction. Living in the country where you have to chop your own firewood, pump your own water, and do a lot of your own repairing is worth the trouble: the psychiatrists make less profit but life is seldom a bore.

On rainy days while poring through old almanacs, I used to copy down recipes and ancient household hints: trying them out was a constant game of fun. Some friends insisted I was being quaint and nostalgically precious but whenever a problem came up, I usually had the answer. I could cure hiccups, light a proper fire, mend almost anything, predict the weather, get rid of ants, swallows, bees, or boring houseguests. I could tell a fresh egg from a spoiled one, clean spots, fix broken furniture, make paint or glue or whitewash or soap, wines, herb teas, and switchel.

And not least of all, I had the making of this handy little book to be read during rainy days, chock full of things to do. Happy doing!

Eric Sloane,
Warren, Connecticut.

P.S. This haphazard, unindexed rambling of things to do, happens to be part of the format; it is just as I copied them down, just as they were in old almanacs and diaries. One book of 1785 tells "how to amputate an arm" and to "remove a gangrenous finger." In the same book, indeed only ten pages later, there are recipes for baking cookies and instructions for the best way to take rust from iron pots. That was often the way information was compiled, and like it or not, it is the way I've put this little book together.

DO
A Little Book of
EARLY AMERICAN
KNOW-HOW

Do hammer a squared peg into a round hole when you wish a wood joint to stay.

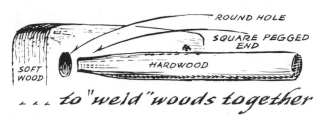

ROUND HOLE

SQUARE PEGGED END

SOFT WOOD

HARDWOOD

... *to "weld" woods together*

A hardwood stick, if partly squared, will soon "weld" itself into a round-holed softwood piece and stay tight throughout the years.

Do use leather from old belts to make small door hinges. Great grandfather used two, three, or four leather pieces on cabinet doors, using tacks or screws; this made silent, easy swinging hinges.

11

Do hang a broom from a nail instead of resting it upon the floor. Letting a broom stand can give it a permanent warp within a few hours.

Do keep a bag of salt as a handy fire extinguisher. A chimney fire can be dealt with by shutting doors and putting salt upon the fire in the grate. Salt-formed gases tend to extinguish flames.

Do measure anything tall (such as a building or tree) by simply measuring its shadow at a given time. By placing a stick in the ground and waiting until its shadow length equals its own height, all other objects' shadows will at that instant also equal their height.

Do pack fancy frosted cakes (for mailing) in popped corn. The icing will smear less but even when it does, the icing will simply produce a sweetened popcorn, good to eat.

Do roll newspapers into rolls by wrapping them with string. A stack of these "logs" will do almost as well in your fireplace as real wood. Newsprint is produced from wood anyway.

Do make a simple fire-maker by filling a lard can with fireplace ashes soaked with kerosene. Supplied with a large spoon, this stuff starts a fire quickly. The Indians in New Mexico still use this as their fire-kindler.

Do before sweeping a floor, sprinkle it with damp tea leaves or bran. This collects dust and also keeps it from rising into the room.

Do trim glass to be made round or oval by cutting it with scissors under water. First mark the oval with a crayon, then with a large scissors cut the glass while it is well submerged. Splinters are less dangerous when kept from flying about, but great care is still necessary.

Do clean woodwork marred by match-scratching etc., by rubbing it with half a lemon. Fingermarks will also disappear by this method.

Do try the simplest of sickroom disinfectants—a plate full of sliced onions.

Do bottle a good woodwork cleaner by saving tea leaves and steeping them in a tin pail for about half an hour. This also washes windows and mirrors with a harmless detergent effect.

Do instead of removing burned-down candle stubs, just place a new candle on the still burning stub. Pressing a new candle over the old stub will firm it in place and save both time and wax.

Do use charcoal as a superb toothcleaner and breath-freshener. Second best is salt, then bicarbonate of soda, all three have been used for centuries. Benjamin Franklin made a mixture of honey and pulverized charcoal for whitening the teeth. Another tooth cleaner recipe was: take a pound of soft water, two ounces of lemon juice, six grains of burnt alum and the same of salt. Boil them for a minute, then strain and bottle for use. Dip a small sponge in this and rub the teeth once a week for removing stains.

Do clean windows with damp newspaper. The ink actually aids in cleaning and the paper is unusually absorbent.

Do keep corrugated cardboard boxes for storing things. Boxes of kindling are easier to pile than loose sticks. A corru-

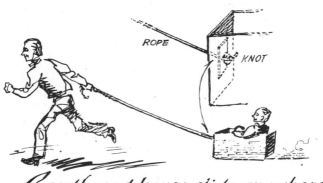

ROPE

KNOT

Cardboard boxes slide anywhere

gated box on the end of a rope makes a fine sled for small children sliding over snow, grass, or land.

Do make candles burn slower (as when a night light is needed) by putting salt on top till it reaches the black part of the wick. In this way the smallest candle can be made to last longer with a steady, mild light.

Do treat infection by piling a pinch of Epsom salts on the infected spot, covering with a bandage, and wetting well. Overnight the infection will be drawn to a head and the surrounding skin soft and fresh.

Do discourage flies by putting out a plate containing half a teaspoon of black pepper, a teaspoon of brown sugar, and a teaspoon of cream. This strange recipe of the 1700's has no logic but seems to work.

Do beat eggs quicker by adding a pinch of salt. Salt cools eggs and produces a quicker froth.

Do move heavy objects (such as an icebox, trunk, etc.) by tipping it onto a

broom. Another person pulling the broom-
handle, the heaviest object may be slid
across the floor with ease.

Do tighten sagging cane-bottom chairs
by turning them upside down and spong-
ing the cane with hot soapy water; then
dry in the sun. Sagging will soon disappear.

Do (in building a house) try fitting the
doorframe to the door instead of fitting
a door into a doorframe. Even a warped
door can be perfectly fitted if it is hung
or put in place and the frame built
around it. No alterations are needed; it's
how the early builders did it.

Do restore withered flowers by plung-
ing the stems into boiling water. By the
time the water is cooled, the flowers will
have been revived. With stems cut off
and left to stand in cold water, they
should then keep for several days.

Do split elm logs by slicing them
around the sides. An axe stuck into the

center of an elm log will become locked in place, and not split the log.

..to split Elm...

Do stain floors with permanganate of potash (drugstores have it) with a quarter ounce to the quart of water. Repeat to darken. At first the color will be bright magenta, but it will soon turn a proper dark brown.

Do use your outstretched arms to measure a room, etc. Fingertip to fingertip your armspread will equal your exact height. Try it and see.

Do make a simple soap by using potatoes three-fourths boiled and then mashed. This not only cleans hands as well as common soap but it prevents winter chap and makes the hands soft and healthy.

Do clean oil paintings with a paste of soft wood ashes and white wine. Quickly add olive oil before wetness soaks into the paint, and use only small amounts.

Do banish odor of onions on the breath by chewing fresh walnuts or a few raw parsley leaves.

Do clean and polish knives with fireplace ashes.

Do unwarp boards with wetness and/or heat. Wood, cardboard or other panels expands on its wet side (or heated side) curling downward. Simply wet or heat the opposite side for a while, and the board will straighten. A board curled from laying on the ground will straighten simply by reversing it (still on the ground) until the warp disappears.

Do know the Weather

Do know the weather and predict it the old fashioned way. For example, a heavy dew at night foretells a clear morrow; a dry night lawn predicts rain on the morrow. When smoke rises quickly, good weather prevails, but when smoke curls downward and lingers near the fire, a storm awaits. Lightning appearing from a western quadrant (southwest, west, or northwest) is from a storm which will reach you, but from any other direction, it is from a storm which will not reach you. A halo around the sun or moon (except in mid-winter) foretells a long, slow precipitation within ten hours. The slower and longer a storm takes to reach you, the longer it will last. Birds flying particularly high indicate cool dry air and good weather.

Do make New England glazed whitewash by taking two gallons of water, a
pound and a half of rice and a pound of
moist sugar. Let this mixture boil until
the rice is dissolved, then thicken it to
a proper consistency with finely powdered
lime. This whitewash gives a lasting
satiny finish seen in the earliest farmhouse walls. By adding milk or eggs the
paint becomes plastic and more lasting.

Do make black paint from an ancient
recipe by baking potatoes (first slowly
and then briskly) until they are com-
pletely burned or charred. This black
powder ground well in linseed oil produces a fine black paint.

Do stop coughing from a cold by roast-
ing a large lemon (without burning it):
when thoroughly hot, cut and squeeze it
into a cup over three ounces of finely
powdered sugar. Take a spoonful to stop
the cough. Another ancient remedy is a
boiled concoction of sugar-water and
pine tree leaves. Plain hoarseness is re-
lieved by a syrup of fresh-scraped horse-
radish and twice its weight in vinegar.

21

Do insure stability with three legs instead of four on tables and benches. Outdoor pieces, small benches, and candle stands were always made with three legs so they would not wobble or upset on old-time uneven floors.

Do pick special apples to be kept for a long while, with cotton gloves. The oil from human hands hastens decay. Lay apples in hay rather than a hard basket, as the slightest bruise also hastens decay.

Do discourage ants by placing cucumber rind shavings wherever they appear.

Do handle fine firearms touching only the wooden parts. Each fingerprint will become a rust spot in time.

Do cure a head cold and hoarseness of the throat with gruel (or oatmeal) made in the regular way: when nearly ready, slice in two or three onions and simmer it for twenty minutes. Pour in a lump of butter with pepper and salt. Eat this with bread and butter (if you are that hungry) before retiring.

Do keep potatoes from sprouting by placing an apple amongst them. The legend is that above-ground plants do not grow together with below-ground plants, and the presence of the above-ground fruit paralyses the growth of the potato.

Do make early American "kitchen red" paint by mixing Indian red or powdered red earth mixed with black from a lamp and binded with sour milk. Milk was a source of the earliest paints and its lasting quality founded the first plastic paints.

Do water newly planted trees by boring holes near the roots, filling holes with water once a week for a month.

Do divide anything into any number of irregular parts by using a ruler. By simply slanting your ruler and still using the inch measurements, you get even more accurate measurements than using arithmetic. For example, it seems difficult to divide a board ten and three-sixteenth inches wide into six parts. But by slanting a one-foot ruler from one side of the board to the other, and then dividing the twelve-inch ruler into six parts, you solve the problem without arithmetic.

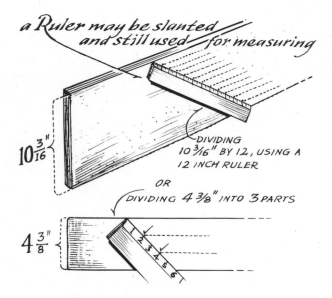

a Ruler may be slanted and still used for measuring

$10\frac{3}{16}''$

DIVIDING
$10\frac{3}{16}''$ BY 12, USING A
12 INCH RULER

OR

DIVIDING $4\frac{3}{8}''$ INTO 3 PARTS

$4\frac{3}{8}''$

Do cure wounds in trees with a paste made of a fourth of lime (old plaster or lime rubbish ground fine will do), a fourth wood ashes, a fourth sand, and a fourth of cow dung. Cow dung alone was also used.

24

Do dry towels in the sun after washing them. Even after ironing wet towels, the slightest dampness evolves into a minute but dangerous mold which is banished by the sun's rays. The old-timers placed their towels on green bushes to dry.

Do keep apples very much longer by not allowing one apple to touch the other. For keeping special apples throughout a winter, wipe them dry and pack them in sawdust, dry sand, or charcoal; then put them in a cool place.

Do ease earache by removing the heart of a roasted onion and placing it into (but not too far) the ear. A stick of green walnut or hickory laid on a fire till the sap ran out the end produced a liquid that early doctors dropped into infected ears. A vinegar and salt wash applied warm was also used.

Do make a good and simple easel for painting by using a ladder. A folding ladder makes a sturdy easel by putting nails at the proper height to hold your canvas or board.

Do put fenceposts into the ground root-end up to prevent rotting. Charring that part to go underground will further prevent damprot.

Do keep salt flowing during damp weather by placing a small cube of soft wood in the salt cellar.

Do remember that the oldest, cheapest, and best toilet powder is simple kitchen starch. You may perfume it to taste with aromatic flowers or herbs pressed into the starch between folded paper.

Do try the oldest recipe for fine hair shampoo and hair softener. Just beat up a fresh egg and rub it into the hair. It sounds messy and takes four washes to complete the shampoo, but it is effective.

Do see objects easier in the dark by looking to just one side of the object. Try looking at a faint star (you can stare it into invisibility); then look to just one side of the star and see it suddenly come into the clearest view.

Do make clothes hooks or shelf brackets from small tree crotches. The oldtimers knew that the strongest part of wood was the crotches of stems, so that is how they made their harness hooks and shelf brackets.

a natural Bracket and Hook

Do keep a bottle of handy spot-remover made of salt and lemon and water. Wet stained cloth with this and allow the material to dry in sunlight. This is also a fine hand conditioner.

Do tell a hard-boiled egg (or a bad egg) from a fresh egg by spinning it. The fresh egg will not spin but wobble to a stop.

Do cure quinsy sore throat with bicarbonate of soda. Make a paper funnel, put a small pinch of powder inside, aim it at the lower throat, and get someone to blow into the funnel.

Do make your own furniture polish. Here are five old-time recipes: 1. A pint bottle filled with equal parts of linseed oil and kerosene; apply with one flannel, dry with another. 2. One pint of linseed oil and a small glass of gin, add half a pound of treacle (sugar-house molasses). If rubbed dry, the shine is remarkable. 3. Three parts linseed oil and one part turpentine; apply with one flannel and dry with another. 4. Mix boiling linseed oil with white varnish (one-fourth varnish and three-fourths oil). 5. One-third vinegar and one-third sweet oil and one-third spirits of wine; shake well and keep for a while.

Do exterminate crawling insects with powdered borax. Another way is to put alum into hot water and boil till it dissolves; then apply to cracks, etc. with no danger to pets or humans.

DO *make old-time* TOYS

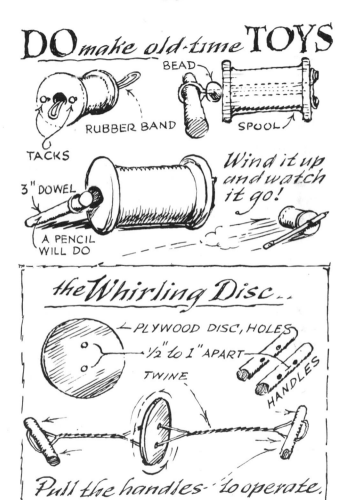

BEAD

RUBBER BAND

SPOOL

TACKS

3" DOWEL

A PENCIL WILL DO

Wind it up and watch it go!

the Whirling Disc

← PLYWOOD DISC, HOLES
½" to 1" APART

TWINE

HANDLES

Pull the handles to operate.

Do get rid of swallows in barns or garages by placing a stuffed owl there. The result is instantaneous and swallows will never return.

Do relieve bee stings with table salt (rubbed into the sting). Ammonia is second best. If neither is available, use mud.

Do remember that house plants enjoy many human foods. Leftover fish, coffee grounds, water from boiled eggs, crushed eggshells, water from cooked foods, watered milk, all give plants a lift. The effects of shrimp is best of any plant reviver.

Do relieve toothache with cloves (powdered or whole).

Do make old-time black schoolroom ink. Half an ounce of logwood and ten grains of bichromate of potash dissolved in a quart of hot rain water. When cold, put into a bottle for a week when it will be ready for use.

Do make a child's hammock from abandoned barrel staves. Placing the staves between separated rope about

two inches apart, a serviceable swinging hammock will result to please the children.

Do hide valuables or cash to protect it from fire while you are away from home for a short while by placing it in a cellophane bag and putting in the freezer. It will be well-hidden and in about the last place to melt from heat. The idea is older than you might think: farmers used to keep paper money in their cold cellars or in the wellhouse, hence the reference to "cold cash."

Do tell where the nearest low pressure area (storm) is located. Just face the wind and hold out your right hand, pointing to your right; you will be pointing toward the nearest storm area. By doing this you can follow the eye of a hurricane as it moves along.

Do build a stump puller or "log jack." Small bushes or tree stumps may be lifted from the earth (in wet weather) by means of a short round log through which has been put an iron rod (a hickory or ash stick might do). A rope used to be used to pull the iron rod, using ox power.

to Pull a Stump

Do make a Paul Revere barn lantern by punching holes in a lard can and putting a candle inside. A good outside

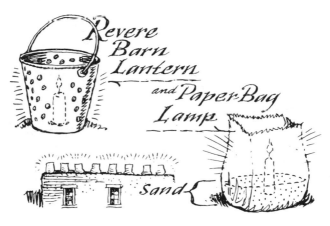

Revere Barn Lantern and Paper-Bag Lamp
Sand

lantern to light a doorway (or for decoration) may be made by partially filling a paper bag with sand and inserting a candle in the bag. In Mexico, Christmas Eves were lit by hundreds of these "candlerias" outlining each house.

Do remove white spots (from hot dishes) on a table by pouring kerosene on the spot, rubbing hard with soft cloth; then pour a bit of wine on it and rub dry.

Do know how to make a perfect oval of any proportion. With two pins, tie a loose loop of thread or cord around them; then holding a pencil upright on the inside of the loop, describe as near a circle as you can, stretching the loop with the pencil as you go. The result will be an oval. Different distances apart of the pins and different size loops will make differently shaped ovals.

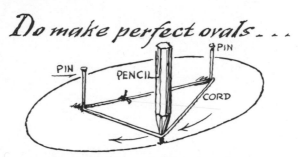

Do make perfect ovals...

FARTHER APART *the* PINS, THINNER *the* OVAL

Do orient yourself at night by knowing that the moon travels about the same course as the sun. A full moon, for example, is always opposite the western setting sun, so it rises in the east.

Do know how to make a five-pointed star, the same way Betsy Ross made the American flag stars to show George Washington, with a scissored piece of white paper.

Do make a 5 pointed Star

① FOLD a SQUARE SHEET. ② FOLD SO,

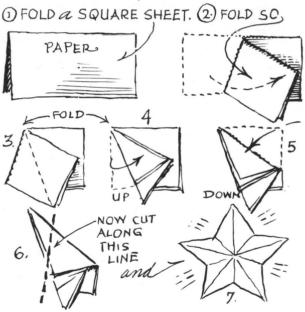

PAPER

FOLD

3.

4.

UP

5.

DOWN

6.

NOW CUT ALONG THIS LINE
and

7.

Do observe clouds and the sky without glare. Paint the underside of a piece of glass black, then look at the reflection of the sky from the top. This "black glass" was used by early artists when painting the sky.

Do make apple butter by stirring it continuously for at least seven hours (which seems to be the old-time trick for excellent butter). They used to use a monstrous iron pot and an eight-foot long wooden "hoe" (for stirring) to keep the farmwife from the intense heat. Mix one gallon of cider and three pounds of sugar, adding spices to taste (allspice, cloves, and cinnamon). Boil to the consistency of molasses and add this mixture to the previously peeled and cubed apples, cooking till it thickens to a creamy consistency.

Do dye your own linens. Tea grounds boiled in iron and set with copperas makes "Williamsburg slate" color. Cloth boiled in heavy tea becomes a rich cream color. Old nails or rusty iron boiled in vinegar with a small bit of alum makes a fine purple slate color. The scaly moss from rocks boiled in water for four hours makes a dye-water if cloth is then boiled till color is correct. Elderberry juice infusion produces blue, tincture of saffron (or nitrate of copperas) produces green, redwood produces red.

Do make your own dandelion wine. Three pounds of dandelion blooms (no stems), three oranges, three lemons, a cake of yeast, and three and one-half pounds of honey (same amount of sugar will substitute). Boil dandelions, oranges, and lemons in two gallons of water for twenty minutes. Let stand overnight and add yeast and sweetening. Pour into crock and cover with cloth: let stand for two weeks before bottling.

Do make simple mead by boiling three parts of water to one part honey until one-third of the mixture evaporates. Skim, pour into cask, and let stand for a week. By adding boiled raisins and brandy, lemon peel and cinnamon, a compound mead is made: cask should then be filled to top so "working" of the mead may overflow. Allow to overflow till frothing ceases, then store for three months.

Do clean silver the way Paul Revere did. Simply make a paste of baking soda and scrub with a brush. A soft toothbrush will do.

Do prevent sickness from overeating or from eating the wrong food the way George Washington did, and not with the aspirin-base pills of today. Just add hot water in a glass to two teaspoonsful of honey and two teaspoonsful of vinegar.

Do know the value of a compass; a piece of string with a tack on one end and a pencil on the other is sufficient. Instead of arithmetic or a square, the old-timers made square foundations and perfectly square rooms with such a device. Collectors have often wondered why there were few rulers or squares to be found in colonial carpenters' tool kits, yet so many large and small wooden compasses. For a few examples of how the compass was used instead of arithmetic, do observe the following two pages of drawings: whereby squares, right angles, octagons, etc. can be made with a simple compass or a compass-string.

to make *Square* with a Compass

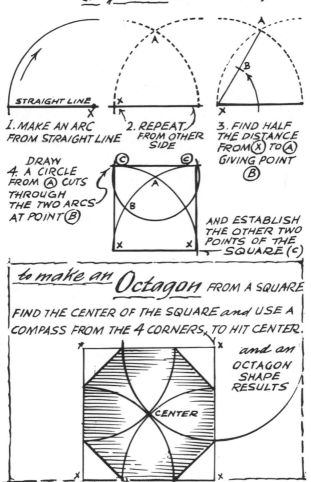

STRAIGHT LINE

1. MAKE AN ARC FROM STRAIGHT LINE

2. REPEAT FROM OTHER SIDE

3. FIND HALF THE DISTANCE FROM (X) TO (A) GIVING POINT (B)

DRAW
4. A CIRCLE FROM (A) CUTS THROUGH THE TWO ARCS AT POINT (B)

AND ESTABLISH THE OTHER TWO POINTS OF THE SQUARE (c)

to make an *Octagon* FROM A SQUARE

FIND THE CENTER OF THE SQUARE *and* USE A COMPASS FROM THE 4 CORNERS, TO HIT CENTER.

and an OCTAGON SHAPE RESULTS

CENTER

to Square board with a Compass...

.. with one end at Ⓐ sweep
an arc through point Ⓧ
to be squared

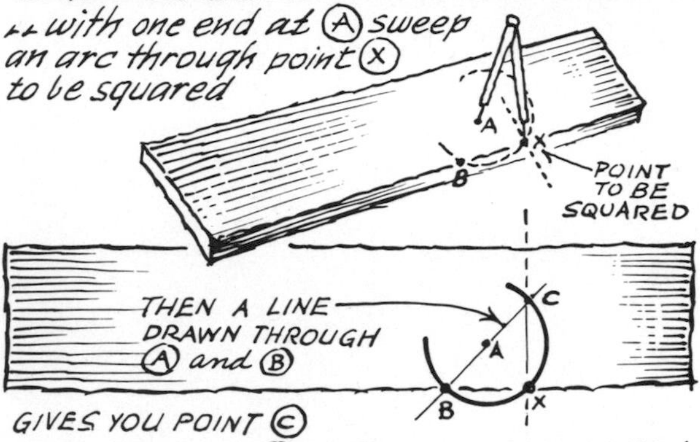

POINT
TO BE
SQUARED

THEN A LINE
DRAWN THROUGH
Ⓐ and Ⓑ

GIVES YOU POINT Ⓒ
AND A LINE FROM Ⓧ TO Ⓒ WILL BE SQUARED !

Do MAKE "Hex" SIGNS WITH A COMPASS...

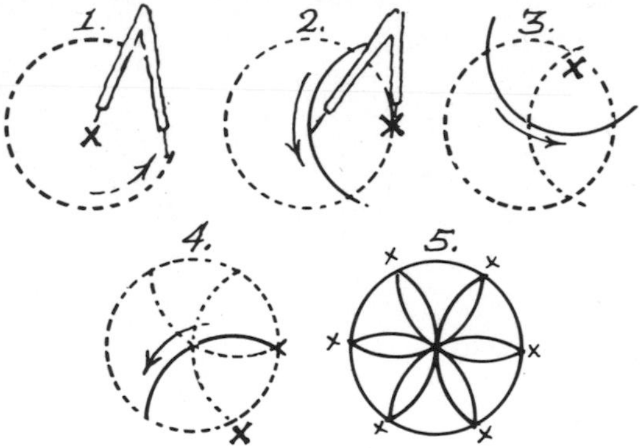

1.

2.

3.

4.

5.

A COMPASS (OR A HAY-FORK) DID THE JOB !

Do make a kitchen porch herb-barrel. Make as many large holes as you can in an old barrel, filling it with stones in the center and rich soil around the outer perimeter. Herbs planted in each hole will thrive and grow outward, being both decorative and useful near the kitchen.

Do mark special books by putting your name or initials unremovable on the bare page-ends instead of on a flat page which could be torn out. Not to be recommended, of course, for rare books.

41

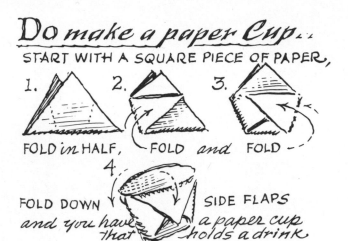

Do make a paper Cup..

START WITH A SQUARE PIECE OF PAPER,

1. FOLD *in* HALF,   2. FOLD *and*   3. FOLD - -

4. FOLD DOWN   SIDE FLAPS
and you have that   *a paper cup holds a drink*

Do make ornamental pyramids out of thick magazines. Discarded Sears and Roebuck catalogs used to be folded page by page, making colorful table decorations of fluted pages, sometimes used as doorstops. One way to use time during long winter snows, this is a slow piece of work but the result will amaze you. A small book (one hundred pages or so) will make a good file for bills, envelopes, etc.

42

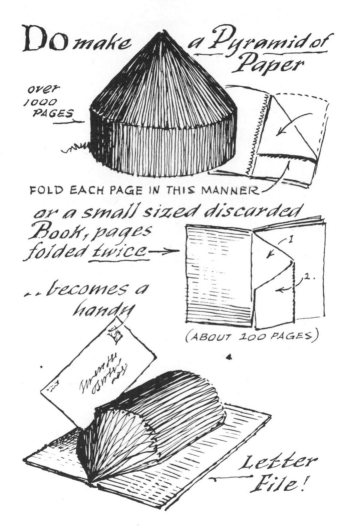

Do *make* a *Pyramid of Paper*

over 1000 PAGES

FOLD EACH PAGE IN THIS MANNER

or a small sized discarded Book, pages folded twice →

1.
2.

(ABOUT 200 PAGES)

..becomes a handy

Letter File!

Do make a boomerang with two sticks. Balsa is best, as a small, light boomerang will circle within a large room. Throw

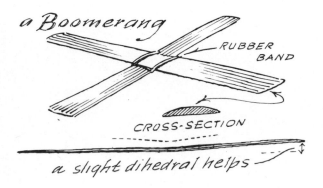

a Boomerang

RUBBER BAND

CROSS-SECTION

a slight dihedral helps

it straight ahead (as if chopping) with a downward hatchet stroke, with the curved side to your left (if you are right-handed), and throw it into the wind. It will return to your hands.

Do make the best skin toner. Make a pint of very strong mint tea, letting it steep overnight. Add one pint of pure apple cider vinegar. Bottle and let stand for two days, when it will be ready for use. Do keep a rain barrel if possible, for rainwater is best for washing ladies' faces and hair.

Do take an air bath. Benjamin Franklin rose each morning at daybreak, got out of bed and passed half an hour in his chamber without any clothes. This, he said, refreshened as much as a complete bath in water.

Do make ginger wine. Five gallons of water and seven pounds of sugar and the whites of four eggs (well beaten and strained) all mixed together while cold. When it boils, skim it well and add at least a quarter pound of common white ginger; then boil for twenty minutes. Have ready the rinds of four lemons cut very thin and pour the hot liquid over them. When cool, put into a cask and add a spoonful of yeast. Next day stop the cask up and bottle within three weeks. Let bottles stand for two to three months.

Do use hay on icy steps during winter, instead of salt or sand. It won't track white spots into the house or poison vegetation. Great-grandfather used to keep a couple of bales of hay beside the farmhouse entrance and scatter a few handfuls of hay around an icy doorway.

Do make a window sundial. Few very early pioneer houses had clocks; and when a clock stopped there was no way to set it when neighbors were far away. The shadow of any upright mullion in a southerly window will cast enough of a shadow on the windowsill to indicate the passing of time, and a very thin pencil line on the sill can show several midday hours, as did many a colonial southerly windowsill.

Do make a barometer with a wide-mouthed bottle, and a piece of toy balloon rubber. By fastening a piece of rubber over the mouth of a wide-mouthed bottle, you will trap the air of the moment inside, with that exact pressure of the day. Lowering outside pressure or rising out-

side pressure will then expand or depress
the rubber cover. By gluing a "pointer"
(a long light sliver of wood or straw) to

MILK
BOTTLE

FAIR

the
Barometer

RAIN

one side of the rubber cover, the pointer
will move up or down according to
weather pressure-changes. This gadget
must be kept from direct sunlight or
other heat which might cause the air
inside to expand or contract from heat
or cold. Even if not very accurate, this
homemade machine explains the action
and mechanics of the modern aneroid
barometer.

Do preserve plants from frost by treating them before being exposed to the sun or thawed. Sprinkle well with spring water in which common salt has been dissolved. Sprinkle again as the plant revives.

Do strike damp matches on glass. A rough surface will crumble match heads but a glass or other smooth surface will usually produce a flame from a damp match.

Do tell the exact temperature by counting the chirps of the common black house cricket. Count the number of chirps occurring in fourteen seconds and then add forty; the result will be the exact temperature (where the cricket is).

Do make gunpowder by mixing five parts of saltpeter with one part of sulphur and one part of charcoal. Mixed with a few drops of water in a mortar, this was rolled in paste rods the thickness of a pin, then cut into small grains and dried.

Do know that one reason for the long fringe on old-time buckskin hunting coats was that in an emergency, each piece of fringe could become a string tied together to produce a longer cord for binding to make a tourniquet or for repairing broken gear.

Do loosen rust stains with salt and lemon juice, then wash off.

Do decorate children's parties with toy balloons. By rubbing the balloon a few times, electric magnetism evolves and the balloon will stick to the wall or ceiling as if by magic. Do not leave the balloon there too long however, as the magnetism attracts dust too, and it will leave a dark ring upon the ceiling.

Do save chimney soot as an extraordinary plant manure. Mixed with a third earth and a third dung, you have a rare medicine for sick plants.

Do recognize true north as the side of a tree trunk with most moss.

Do Know how to bind with both ends of the binding underneath.

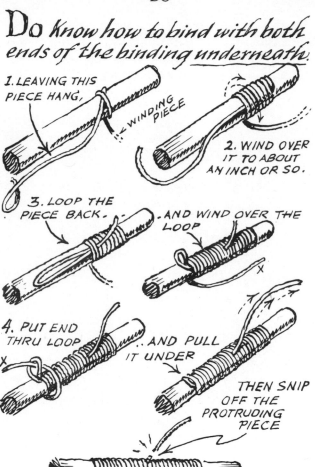

1. LEAVING THIS PIECE HANG,

WINDING PIECE

2. WIND OVER IT TO ABOUT AN INCH OR SO.

3. LOOP THE PIECE BACK.

AND WIND OVER THE LOOP

4. PUT END THRU LOOP

AND PULL IT UNDER

THEN SNIP OFF THE PROTRUDING PIECE

SILK·BOUND FISH·POLES WERE DONE THIS WAY.

Do ease stuck drawers or windows with common brown soap. It makes the best and longest-lasting wood lubricant.

Do try these 1749 dessert recipes...

PIPPIN TARTS. Pare thin, two oranges; boil the peels tender and shred fine. Core and pare twenty apples and put them in a stew pan with as little water as possible to cook. When half done add half a pound of sugar, the orange juice and the peel, and boil till thick. When cold, put in shallow dish to be eaten cold.

SYLLABUBS. Mix a quart of thick raw cream, a pound of sugar, a pint of white and a pint of sweet wine in a deep pan. Add the grated peels and the juice of three lemons. Beat or whisk it one way half an hour, then put in glasses. It will keep for ten days in a cool place.

ORANGE FOOL. Mix the juice of three oranges, a pint of cream, a little nutmeg and cinnamon, and sweeten to taste. Set the whole over a slow fire and stir till it becomes as thick as melted butter, but it must not be boiled. Pour it into a dish for eating cold.

LEMON HONEYCOMB. Sweeten the juice of a lemon to your taste and put it into a dish. Mix the white of an egg with a pint of rich cream and a little sugar; whisk it and as the froth rises, put it into the dish and over the lemon juice. Do this the day before it is to be used.

POTATO CHEESECAKES. Boil six ounces of potatoes and (separately) four ounces of lemon peel; beat the latter in a mortar with four ounces of sugar; then add the potatoes, beaten, and four ounces of butter melted in a little cream. When well mixed, let it stand to cool. Put crust in pattypans and rather more than half fill them. Bake in a quick oven half an hour. Sprinkle sugar on them when going to the oven.

SACK CREAM. Boil a pint of raw cream, the yelk (yolk) of an egg well beaten, three teaspoons of white wine, sugar and lemon peel to taste. Stir over a gentle fire till it be as thick as rich cream. Put in a dish to be served cold with rusks or sippets of toasted bread.

QUICK PUDDING. Flour and suet half a pound each, four eggs, a quarter pint of new milk, a little mace and nutmeg, a quarter pound of raisins, ditto of currants. Mix well and boil three quarters of an hour with lid on the pot.

The 1800s